Alphabet Songs & Rhymes

Table of Contents

A...4
B...7
C...10
D...13
E...16
F...19
G...22
H...25
I...28
J...31
K...34
L...37
M...40
N...43
O...46
P...49
Q...52
R...55
S...58
T...61
U...64
V...67
W...70
X...73
Y...75
Z...78

www.themailbox.com

©2004 by THE EDUCATION CENTER, INC.
All rights reserved.
ISBN# 1-56234-604-0

Manufactured in the United States
10 9 8 7 6 5 4 3 2

Alphabet
Songs & Rhymes
By Jean Warren

Literacy for Little Learners

Managing Editor: Susan Walker

Editorial Team: Becky S. Andrews, Kimberley Bruck, Karen P. Shelton, Diane Badden, Susan Walker, Kimberly A. Brugger, Cindy Daoust, Leanne Stratton, Allison E. Ward, Karen A. Brudnak, Sarah Hamblet, Hope Rodgers, Dorothy C. McKinney

Production Team: Lisa K. Pitts, Kimberly Richard (COVER ARTIST), Pam Crane, Clevell Harris, Rebecca Saunders, Jennifer Tipton Bennett, Chris Curry, Theresa Lewis Goode, Ivy L. Koonce, Clint Moore, Greg D. Rieves, Barry Slate, Donna K. Teal, Tazmen Carlisle, Amy Kirtley-Hill, Kristy Parton, Debbie Shoffner, Cathy Edwards Simrell, Lynette Dickerson, Mark Rainey

Why use songs and rhymes to strengthen alphabet knowledge?

Saying rhymes and singing songs is just plain fun. But that's not all. Rhymes, spoken or sung, nurture listening skills and encourage creative uses of language. Songs stimulate the brain, engaging children in a unique way and helping them remember things that might otherwise easily slip from memory. Singing even helps develop important early literacy skills such as phonemic awareness. But perhaps the best reason for using lots of songs and rhymes with three-, four-, and five-year-olds is that **children love them so much!**

About This Book

This book is packed with oodles of kid-pleasing songs and rhymes—just perfect for familiarizing children with letters, sounds, and related words.

Alphabetically Arranged

Songs and rhymes are arranged in order alphabetically according to the letter emphasized.

Pick and Choose

You can pick and choose with confidence because all the songs are sung to familiar tunes and incorporate common themes.

Extras to Enhance Learning

To add an extra special touch, some verses are accompanied by suggestions for enhancing learning. Others come with tips for simply adding to the singing, rhyming, and letter-knowledge fun!

Extending the Learning

You will find many ways to adapt and use the songs and rhymes in this book. Consider extending learning experiences in the following ways:
- making song charts
- making big books
- making individual books for children
- having children act out the songs and rhymes

A

I Love A words

Introduce your students to words that begin with short *A* using this short familiar tune.

(sung to the tune of "Skip to My Lou")

I love *A* words; how about you?
I love *A* words, yes I do.
I love *A* words. Here are a few:
Apples, ants, and *alligators* too!

Repeat the song, substituting other short A *words.*

A Sounds

These kid-pleasing lyrics will draw students' attention to both the long and short *A* sounds. You can bet they'll be singing this tune long after your lesson ends!

(sung to the tune of "Jingle Bells")

A, A, A, A, A, A
*A*s are all around.
We would all like to know—
What is *A*'s short sound?

/ă/, /ă/, /ă/, /ă/, /ă/, /ă/
/ă/ is what we say.
Do you know any words
That start the short *A* way?

Children's chant:
Apple, ant, and *alligator* too
Start with short *A*, yes they do!

Repeat the song, substituting different short A *words in the chant. Or use the next verse to practice long* A.

A, A, A, A, A, A
*A*s are all around.
We would all like to know—
What is *A*'s long sound?

/ā/, /ā/, /ā/, /ā/, /ā/, /ā/
/ā/ is what we say.
Do you know any words
That start the long *A* way?

Children's chant:
Ape, acorn, and *April* too
Start with long *A*, yes they do!

Hooray!

When You See an A

Gather picture cards for this fun tune and incorporate them into the song. Then keep them handy for a post-singing short *A* picture review.

(sung to the tune of "If You're Happy and You Know It")

When you see an *A* thing, shout, "Hooray!"
When you see an *A* thing, shout, "Hooray!"
Look for apples and astronauts;
Spy some ants and alligators.
There are lots and lots of things that start with *A*.
Hooray!

Repeat the song, substituting different short A *words as desired.*

Astronaut Bear

When a few readings of this poem are complete, have each child draw a picture of a short *A* item that astronaut bear might see from the air. Combine them into a class book for a fun letter-sound review!

Astronaut, astronaut, astronaut bear,
Waving at planes up in the air.

Astronaut, astronaut, astronaut bear,
Spotting *A* things from up there.

Anchors, apples, and little ants too.
Down on earth, there are quite a few.

Let's Look for A Today

(sung to the tune of "The Farmer in the Dell")

Let's look for *A* today.
Let's look for *A* today.
Heigh-ho, away we go.
Let's look for *A* today.

Ant starts with *A*.
Apple starts with *A*.
Alligator and *applesauce,*
They both start with *A*.

We See A Things

Before beginning this simple song, place several short *A* items plus a few non-*A* items in the center of your circle-time area. Then seat your students around the objects. While singing the song, substitute four students' names in the last four lines and have each child locate and pick up a short *A* item. Action!

(sung to the tune of "Are You Sleeping?")

We see *A* things.
We see *A* things.
Yes, we do!
Yes, we do!
[Child's name], pick up one thing.
[Child's name], pick up one thing.
[Child's name] too!
[Child's name] too!

I'm a Beautiful Bumblebee

After students are familiar with this rhyme, play this fun follow-up game. To prepare, draw or glue pictures of *B* and non-*B* words to paper flower cutouts. Secure the flowers to the floor. Ask students to scurry around the room like bees while they recite the rhyme. When the rhyme ends, have each student stop on a flower only if it shows a *B* picture. They'll be buzzing for more!

I'm a beautiful bumblebee.
I land on things that start with *B*:
Bunny and basket,
Butter and bread.
And when I'm tired,
I go to bed!

Let's Look for Bs Today

Students seek and find the letter *B* with this little ditty! After singing the song, have youngsters search the room for the letter *B*.

(sung to the tune of "The Farmer in the Dell")

Let's look for *B*s today.
Let's look for *B*s today.
Heigh-ho, just watch us go.
Let's look for *B*s today.

We found one on a block;
We found one in a book.
Heigh-ho, just watch us go.
We found some *B*s today.

The Bees on the Boat

Youngsters are all abuzz with this song and idea for the letter *B*! Write the song on a chart. Give each child a sticky note labeled with an uppercase or a lowercase *B*. As you sing the song, point to each child and have him place his sticky note over the corresponding letter on the chart. Buzzzz!

(sung to the tune of "The Wheels on the Bus")

Oh, the bees on the boat
Go buzz, buzz, buzz,
Buzz, buzz, buzz,
Buzz, buzz, buzz.
Oh, the bees on the boat
Go buzz, buzz, buzz.
Please let them off!

The bees on the boat,
They say, "Bye-bye,"
Say, "Bye-bye,"
Say, "Bye-bye."
The bees on the boat,
They say, "Bye-bye,"
And off they fly!

Bears Going to the Fair

Youngsters become dancing bear cubs when they act out this little ditty!

(sung to the tune of "Twinkle, Twinkle, Little Star")

Black bear, black bear
Brushes her hair.
She is going to the fair.
She will ride a bumper boat.
She will bob for apples that float.
She will buy two big balloons.
She will boogie to some tunes.

Pretend to brush hair.
Walk in place.
Pretend to steer boat.
Pretend to bob for apples.
Pretend to hold balloon strings.
Dance.

Brown bear, brown bear,
Brushes his hair.
He is going to the fair.
He will eat some berry pie.
He will bounce up in the sky.
He will smash some water balloons.
He will boogie to some tunes.

Pretend to brush hair.
Walk in place.
Pretend to eat pie.
Jump in place.
Pretend to toss water balloons.
Dance.

Baker Bear

There's a whole lot of letter tracing going on with this activity and rhyme. Write the rhyme on a chart. After reciting it, invite youngsters to use a blue highlighter to trace over each *B* on the chart.

Baker, baker,
Baker bear
Bakes berry pies
For the fair.

Blueberry, blackberry,
Boysenberry too.
I'll have blueberry!
How about you?

I Love B words

(sung to the tune of "Skip to My Lou")

I love *B* words; how about you?
I love *B* words; yes, I do.
I love *B* words. Here's a few:
Baby, ball, and *bananas* too!

Repeat the song, substituting other B *words.*

My B Box

Students are eager to make a *B* box after reciting this rhyme. Simply label a large box with the letter *B* and have each child find a *B* item in the room and then place it in the box. Continue the collection, including items students bring from home if desired.

I have a big box.
I colored it blue.
I fill it with *B* things.
I have quite a few.

I have some boats
And some buttons and bows.
I have some balls
That I like to throw.

I take my box
Wherever I go.
I might need a *B* thing.
You just never know!

Three Baby Bunnies

After singing this song a few times, have students practice writing the letter *B* on their own funny money. Draw a simple dollar bill pattern with a *B* in the middle. Make copies so that each student has several. Let students trace the letter *B* onto each bill; then have them use the money for a dramatic presentation of this song.

(sung to the tune of "Three Blind Mice")

Three baby bunnies,
Three baby bunnies,
They're so funny
With their money.
They bought a baseball and a bat.
They bought a bow for a big blue hat.
They bought a beach ball but it went flat.
Three baby bunnies.

C

Clap for C

Gather an assortment of items whose names begin with the hard *C* sound and a few that don't begin with hard *C*. When youngsters have sung the song through, hold up an item and instruct them to clap if it's name begins with hard *C*.

(sung to the tune of "Row, Row, Row Your Boat")

Clap, clap, clap your hands.
Clap your hands for *C*.
When you see a *C* thing,
Clap your hands for me.

C Sounds

These kid-pleasing lyrics will draw students' attention to both the hard and soft *C* sounds. You can bet they'll be singing this tune long after your lesson ends!

(sung to the tune of "Jingle Bells")

C, C, C, C, C, C
*C*s are all around.
We would all like to know—
What is *C*'s hard sound?

/k/, /k/, /k/, /k/, /k/, /k/
/k/ is what we say.
Do you know any words
That start the hard *C* way?

Children's chant:
Cake, color, and *corn* too
Start with /k/; yes, they do!

Repeat the song, substituting different hard C words in the chant. Or use the next verse to practice soft C.

C, C, C, C, C, C
*C*s are all around.
We would all like to know—
What is *C*'s soft sound?

/s/, /s/, /s/, /s/, /s/, /s/
/s/ is what we say.
Do you know any words
That start the soft *C* way?

Children's chant:
Celery, cinnamon, and *circle* too
Start with /s/; yes, they do!

/k/, /k/, /k/,
/k/, /k/, /k/

I Love C Foods

After singing this happy tune, have youngsters draw and label their favorite *C* foods on individual paper plates. Yum!

(sung to the tune of "Skip to My Lou")

I love carrots, yum, yum, yum.
I love cornbread, even crumbs.
I love candy; oh, what fun.
I love *C* foods in my tum!

I love corn, yum, yum, yum.
I love cookies, even crumbs.
I love cupcakes; oh, what fun.
I love *C* foods in my tum!

Cowboy Bear

Little cowpokes can eagerly help this cowboy bear by lassoing *C* words of their own. Program a supply of index cards with hard *C* words or pictures and some with non-*C* words or pictures. Lay a length of yarn on the floor to resemble a lasso. Have each student draw a card, in turn, and then place only a *C* word card in the center of the lasso.

Cowboy, cowboy,
Cowboy bear
Rounds up *C* words everywhere.
Cows, cards, and *corn* too,
Cars and *coins,* to name a few.

11

I Love C words

Grab a stuffed cat toy for this activity. After reciting the rhyme, show children the cat and then have them call out as many *C* words as they can for one to two minutes before the cat runs away (moves behind your back)!

"I love *C* words," said the cat.
"Like *cake* and *cookies*
And words like that."

How many *C* words can you say
Before the cat runs away?

clock

Let's Look for Cs Today

Students seek and find the letter *C* with this little ditty! After singing a couple of rounds of this song, have youngsters search the room for the letter *C*.

*(sung to the tune of
"The Farmer in the Dell")*

Let's look for *C*s today.
Let's look for *C*s today.
Heigh-ho, away we go.
Let's look for *C*s today.

I Love D

(sung to the tune of "Skip to My Lou")

I love doughnuts and dump trucks too.
I love dinosaurs; how about you?
I love dessert when dinner is through.
I love *D.* Oh yes, I do!

D Sounds

(sung to the tune of "Jingle Bells")

D, D, D, D, D, D
Lots of *D*s around.
We would all like to know
How to make your sound.

/d/, /d/, /d/, /d/, /d/, /d/
/d/ is what you say.
We can say a lot of words
That start out this way.

Encourage youngsters to suggest words that begin with the letter D as you write their suggestions on chart paper.

/d/, /d/, /d/, /d/

Dunking Doughnuts!

You'll get requests by the dozens for this sweet little song! Encourage youngsters to listen carefully as they sing. Then invite them to identify words in the song that begin with *D.*

(sung to the tune of "Clementine")

Dunk your doughnut, dunk your doughnut
In the milk that's in your cup.
When it's gotten nice and soggy,
Then it's time to eat it up!

Down on the Farm

Welcome to the *D* farm! Repeat the song with your students, each time substituting a different word that begins with the letter *D* (see the suggestions below).

(sung to the tune of "Old MacDonald Had a Farm")

Dave and Dinah had a farm.
/d/, /d/, /d/, /d/, /d/
And on their farm they had some *D*s.
/d/, /d/, /d/, /d/, /d/
With a [dog] here and a [dog] there.
Here a [dog], there a [dog],
Everywhere a [dog], [dog].
Dave and Dinah had a farm.
/d/, /d/, /d/, /d/, /d/

Suggested words: duck, deer, donkey, desk, dish, door

What Could We See?

Little ones imagine things they could see that begin with the letter *D* when they perform this action rhyme!

D, D, what could we see?	*Point to eyes.*
What could we see that starts with *D?*	*Throw hands outward with palms up.*
We could see daytime with the sun in the sky.	*Make a circle with arms above head.*
We could see ducks as they fly by.	*Flap arms.*
We could see doughnuts so round and sweet.	*Rub tummy.*
We could see the dirt beneath our feet.	*Stomp feet.*

Down by the Duck Pond

Enrich a singing of this ducky little song by reviewing two *D* words found in the lyrics. Write the words *duck* and *ducklings* on chart paper. Invite children to point to the *D* in each word. Then explain that a duckling is a baby duck before diving into the song!

(sung to the tune of "Down by the Station")

Down by the duck pond,
Early in the morning,
See the little ducklings
Swimming in a row.
See the momma duck
So proud of all her ducklings.
Quack, quack, quack, quack.
Off they go!

writing Letter D

Invite each youngster to write a *D* in the air with her index finger as she follows the steps given in this tune!

(sung to the tune of "The Muffin Man")

I love to write the letter *D*,
The letter *D*, the letter *D*.
First go down and then around.
It makes a *D*, you see!

Little Elf

Who better to introduce the sounds of letter *E* than a mischievous little elf? While students are away, stock your circle area with objects whose names begin with *E*, such as an envelope, egg, engine, elephant, and so forth. When students return, ask one student to pretend he's the little elf. Teach students the tune, and then lead them in singing the first verse. Have the little elf sing the second verse and name two of the objects.

(sung to the tune of "Are You Sleeping?")

What do you see
That starts with *E,*
Little elf,
Little elf?

I see an [name of object].
I see an [name of object].
You'll agree;
They start with *E.*

Repeat the song as desired, inviting a different child to name E *objects each time.*

E Sounds

This little ditty will engage your little ones while reinforcing short and long *E.* Excellent!

(sung to the tune of "Jingle Bells")

E, E, E, E, E, E
Lots of *E*s around.
Everyone would like to know—
What's your short *E* sound?

/ĕ/, /ĕ/, /ĕ/, /ĕ/, /ĕ/, /ĕ/
/ĕ/ is what we say.
Do you know of any words
That start the short *E* way?

Children's chant:
Eggs, elf, and *elephant* too
All start with short *e;* yes, they do!

Repeat the song, substituting different long E *words in the chant, or use the next verse to practice short* E.

E, E, E, E, E, E
Lots of *E*s around.
Everyone would like to know—
What's your long *E* sound?

/ē/, /ē/, /ē/, /ē/, /ē/, /ē/
/ē/ is what we say.
Do you know of any words
That start the long *E* way?

Children's chant:
Eagle, Easter, and *eel* too
All start with long *E;* yes, they do!

Engineer Bear

Here's an opportunity for extra practice with short *E*. Write this poem on chart paper, and then ask volunteers to wear an engineer's hat as they point to short *E* words.

Engineer, engineer,
Engineer bear,
Driving your train
From here to there.

Chugging past evergreens
And eggs in a nest.
Chugging past elk
All looking their best.

Chugging past elves
Out in the snow.
Chugging past elephants
In a circus show.

Elevator E

Elevator, elevator, elevator *E,*
Going up to floor number three.

Open the doors, and what do we see?
Only things that start with short *E!*

Engines with engineers, eggs of blue,
Elephants, eggplants, and envelopes too.

Elevator, elevator, elevator *E,*
Going up to floor number three.

Open the doors, and what do we see?
Only things that start with long *E!*

Eagles, eels, and Easter candy,
Easels and erasers—they come in handy!

Elevator, elevator, elevator *E,*
Going up to floor number three.

I Love E Things

Introduce your students to words that begin with long *E* using this short, familiar tune.

(sung to the tune of "Skip to My Lou")

I love *E* words; how about you?
I love *E* words; yes, I do.
I love *E* words. Here are a few:
Eagles, east, and *easels* too!

Repeat the song, substituting other long E *words.*

Let's Look for E Today

(sung to the tune of "The Farmer in the Dell")

Let's look for *E* today.
Let's look for *E* today.
Heigh-ho, away we go.
Let's look for *E* today.

Egg starts with *E.*
Engine starts with *E.*
Elephant and *evergreen,*
They both start with *E.*

Let's Fish for Fs

Singing this *F* song is more fun when you play this simple magnetic fishing game too! On paper fish cutouts, write *F* words, such as *feather, fire, farm,* and *foot.* Then add a corresponding picture. Attach paper clips to the fish and string a magnet to a simple pole. Teach youngsters the first verse below. Then let your children take turns catching fish and reading the *F* words. When a child catches a fish, have her sing the second verse below, substituting her *F* word.

(sung to the tune of "The Farmer in the Dell")

Let's fish for *F*s today.
Let's fish for *F*s today.
Heigh-ho, away we go.
Let's fish for *F*s today.

I caught a [foot] today.
I caught a [foot] today.
Heigh-ho, just watch me go.
I caught a [foot] today.

Four Little Frogs

After your little ones enjoy singing a round of this song, ask volunteers to name other items that begin with *F.* Draw or write the name of each item on chart paper for all to see.

(sung to the tune of "Up on the Housetop")

Four little frogs went fishing one day.
One caught a feather, but it floated away.
One caught a football and threw it high.
One caught a fork just right for pie.

Fee, fie, foe! Watch them go.
Fee, fie, fum! Oh, what fun!
Four little frogs went fishing today.
What else did they catch? Can you say?

Swim Like Fish

Swim, hop, and toss—this movement song is sure to reinforce the *F* sound and get the wiggles out! Teach students the song while modeling fish movements. Then invite everyone to sing and move to the beat together. Ask students to listen for the word that begins with *F* in each phrase.

(sung to the tune of "Clementine")

[Swim like fish],
[Swim like fish],
[Swim like fish] just now.
Just now [swim like fish].
First, I will show you how.

Repeat the song, substituting a different movement verse each time, such as drift like feathers, toss a football, *or* fly like fairies.

Forest Bear

Encourage youngsters to listen for the *F* sound as you read this poem aloud. Ask each child to raise one finger each time he hears /f/. Then read the poem to your group, checking for understanding as you go.

Forest, forest,
Forest bear,
Greeting friends
Everywhere.

Four fast foxes,
Falcons that fly,
Five fine fish
Who passed right by.

Then one day
Bear heard a cry.
There was smoke
Up in the sky.

Bear rang the bell
To call the fire truck,
And soon the firefighters
Arrived; what luck!

They fought the fire
And put it out.
The forest animals
All gave a shout.

"Hip, hip, hooray
For forest bear
And brave firefighters
Everywhere!"

On a Farm

Farm begins with *F.* That's fantastic! Use this song with its simple repetition to help students focus on the word *farm* and its beginning sound /f/. Before singing, copy the song onto chart paper. Then invite volunteers to use a highlighter to circle the *F* words *farm* and *farmer.*

(sung to the tune of "London Bridge Is Falling Down")

Animals live on a farm, on a farm, on a farm.
Animals live on a farm with a farmer.

Cows and pigs live on a farm, on a farm, on a farm.
Cows and pigs live on a farm with a farmer.

Goats and sheep live on a farm, on a farm, on a farm.
Goats and sheep live on a farm with a farmer.

Hens and chicks live on a farm, on a farm, on a farm.
Hens and chicks live on a farm with a farmer.

Firefly, I See Your Light!

These fingertip fireflies will flit to *F* words in your classroom! Invite each child to press a fingertip onto a washable yellow stamp pad and then let his fingertip dry. Sing the song below with your youngsters and have each child use his yellow fingertip as a firefly while he explores the classroom, pointing to all the *F* words he can find. How enlightening!

(sung to the tune of "Shoo Fly")

Firefly, I see your light!
Firefly, I see your light!
Firefly, I see your light!
I see you shine on summer nights!

I'm a Little Gumball

When youngsters have sung this tune several times, invite them to practice writing the letter *G* on colorful gumball cutouts. Tape the gumballs to a large gumball machine cutout. Then display the gumball machine in the classroom. Sweet!

(sung to the tune of "I'm a Little Teapot")

I'm a little gumball
Round and small.
I don't cost very
Much at all.

You can put a penny
In the slot.
Turn the handle
And out I pop!

I Love *G!*

(sung to the tune of "Three Blind Mice")

I love *G.*
I love *G.*
Can't you see?
I love *G.*

I love gorillas at the zoo.
I also love grasshoppers; how about you?
I love to eat gallons of gumdrops too!
I love *G.*
I love *G.*

Writing the Letter *G*

While singing this kid-pleasing tune with your little ones, encourage them to use their index fingers to "write" the letter *G* in the air!

(sung to the tune of "The Muffin Man")

I love to write the letter *G,*
The letter *G,* the letter *G.*
I love to write the letter *G*
For everyone to see!

The Galloping Ghost

Introduce the words that begin with *G* in the lyrics below before your youngsters sing this "spook-tacular" song!

(sung to the tune of "My Bonnie Lies Over the Ocean")

The ghost gallops over the gate.
The ghost gallops over the tree.
The ghost gallops into the garden.
The ghost is hungry, you see!
Hungry, hungry, the ghost is hungry, you see, you see!
Hungry, hungry, the ghost is hungry, you see!

He gobbled up all of the garden,
Then giggled and twirled through the air.
Now we have to go to the grocery
And get all our vegetables there!
Hungry, hungry, the ghost was hungry, you see, you see!
Hungry, hungry, the ghost was hungry, you see!

Out in the Garden

Although gophers tend to be disliked by gardeners, they are perfect for studying the letter *G* in this song!

(sung to the tune of "Down by the Station")

Out in the garden,
Early in the morning,
See the little gopher
Digging all around.

He eats all the plants
And makes the gardener angry.
Then he hides in his tunnel
Under the ground.

Garbage Collection!

Display the words to this petite poem on sentence strips in a pocket chart. Then have youngsters locate words that begin with *G* before reciting the poem.

Garbage, garbage, garbage bear,
He gathers all the garbage everywhere!
His big truck rumbles as it goes down the road,
Stopping at each house to add to its load.

Where Is G?

Invite little ones to perform this song with easy-to-prepare puppets. Make an uppercase and a lowercase stick puppet similar to the ones shown for each child. Then have each student hold a puppet in each hand to perform the song!

(sung to the tune of "Where Is Thumbkin?")

Where is *G?* Where is *G?*	Hold puppets behind back.
Here it is! Here it is!	Reveal one puppet, then the other.
Can you say the *G* sound?	Wiggle one puppet.
Can you say the *G* sound?	Wiggle the other puppet.
/g/, /g/, /g/, /g/, /g/, /g/	Wiggle both puppets.

I Love *H*

(sung to the tune of "Three Blind Mice")

I love *H*.
I love *H*.
H is great.
H is great.

H is for *hot dogs* and *hamburgers* too.
H is hundreds of hugs for you!
H is a hat that is fancy and new.
I love *H*.
I love *H*.

Happy, Healthy, and Hungry!

Help your little ones learn the sound of letter *H* with an action song that focuses on descriptive words!

(sung to the tune of "Clementine")

H is happy;	Point to smile.
H is healthy.	Hold up arms and show muscles.
H is huge, and	Stretch arms far apart.
H is hot.	Fan yourself.
H is hungry;	Rub stomach.
H is handsome.	Place hands on cheeks.
H is helpful;	Find a classmate.
Thanks a lot!	Shake the classmate's hand.

The Hungry Horse

Review the sound of letter *H* with your students before singing this song. Once children have practiced the song several times, divide the students into two groups. Designate one group as horses and the other as farmers. Have the farmers perform the first stanza of the song, and the horses perform the final stanza!

(sung to the tune of "Are You Sleeping")

Hungry horse,
Hungry horse,
Here's your hay.
Here's your hay.

Rub stomach.
Rub stomach.
Pretend to lay hay on the floor.
Pretend to lay hay on the floor.

Happy, happy horse,
Happy, happy horse,
Run and play.
Run and play.

Smile.
Smile.
Run in place.
Run in place.

Hibernating Bear

Youngsters can "bear-ly" contain themselves when they listen to this silly poem! Encourage students to join in as you recite the poem several times. Then explain that everything the bear dreams of begins with the letter *H.* Invite students to suggest other things the bear could dream of that begin with *H.* Then encourage them to draw a picture of a dream for hibernating bear!

Hibernating bear doesn't make a peep.
What does he dream of in his sleep?
Does he dream of happy hikes on a hill?
Does he dream of honey pots he can fill?
Or how about a hippo in a party hat?
No, I'm sure he doesn't dream of that!

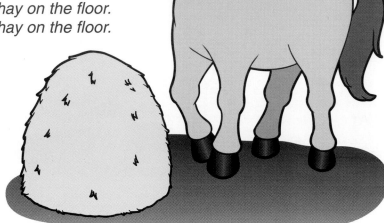

Up, Up, and Away!

Little ones' imaginations soar when they perform this cute song! Before the performance, be sure to have your students repeat the word *helicopter* several times and listen carefully to the sound of letter *H* at the beginning of the word.

(sung to the tune of "I'm a Little Teapot")

I'm a helicopter   Point to self.
On the ground.   Point to ground.
I flip my switch,   Pretend to flip a switch.
And my blades go around.   Twirl around.

When I get all revved up,   Wiggle body.
I can fly   Point to self.
Up, up, up   Point up.
Into the sky.   Pretend to fly around the room.

/h/

A Lovely Sound!

(sung to the tune of "She'll Be Comin' Round the Mountain")

Oh, the letter *H* makes such a lovely sound!
Oh, the letter *H* makes such a lovely sound!
Well, I think we should all try it.
It says /h/. It's very quiet!
Oh, the letter *H* makes such a lovely sound! /h/, /h/

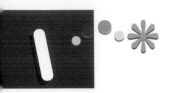

I'm a Little Inchworm

Make a path of picture cards in your classroom. Include pictures of items whose names begin with short *I* (such as *insect, infant,* and *instruments*) and others that don't. Teach your youngsters this silly song; then have them pretend to be inchworms inching past the pictures and nodding to those with names that begin with the short *I* sound.

(sung to the tune of "I'm a Little Teapot")

I'm a little inchworm,
Short and round.
I love to inch
Along the ground.

When I see something
That starts with short *I,*
I nod to it
As I inch by.

I Sounds

This little ditty will engage your little ones while reinforcing short and long *I.* Ideal!

(sung to the tune of "Jingle Bells")

I, I, I, I, I, I
Lots of *I*s around.
Everyone would like to know—
What's your short *I* sound?

/ĭ/, /ĭ/, /ĭ/, /ĭ/, /ĭ/, /ĭ/
/ĭ/ is what we say.
Do you know of any words
That start the short *I* way?

Children's chant:
Insects, inch, and *instrument* too
Start with short *I;* yes, they do!

Repeat the song, substituting different short I words in the chant. Or use the next verse to practice long I.

I, I, I, I, I, I
Lots of *I*s around.
Everyone would like to know—
What's your long *I* sound?

/ī/, /ī/, /ī/, /ī/, /ī/, /ī/
/ī/ is what we say.
Do you know of any words
That start the long *I* way?

Children's chant:
Icicle, idea, and *iron* too
Start with long I; yes, they do!

INVENTOR Bear

Inventing seems to come easy for this little bear! After reading this poem with your little ones, see what inventions they might be inspired to create. Provide building blocks or other construction toys; then give them time to bring their creations to life! Encourage inventions that also begin with the letter *I*. Inventor bear will be proud!

Inventor, inventor,
Inventor bear
Invents short *I* things
Everywhere.

Igloos so small
They only fit mice.
Itty-bitty instruments
The size of rice.

Instant tea
That glows when you drink.
Write in the air
With invisible ink!

Inventor bear
Is quite interesting.
I'd like to meet him
And see these things!

Imagine a Place

Inspire understanding of the short *I* sound when you share this poem with youngsters. After several readings, invite each child to raise her pinky finger whenever she hears the short *I* sound. Then have students brainstorm other short *I* words to create additional verses.

Imagine a place where insects can talk.
Imagine a place where infants can walk.
Imagine a place where instruments play
All by themselves every day.
Imagine a world with interesting sights,
All of them *I* things. What a delight!

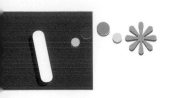

I Love I words

Use this short, familiar tune to introduce your students to words that begin with long *I*.

(sung to the tune of "Skip to My Lou")

I love *I* words; how about you?
I love *I* words; yes, I do.
I love *I* words. Here are a few:
Icicle, iron, and *ivy* too!

*Repeat the song, substituting other long
I words.*

Let's Look for I Today

*(sung to the tune of
"The Farmer in the Dell")*

Let's look for *I* today.
Let's look for *I* today.
Heigh-ho, away we go.
Let's look for *I* today.

Ink starts with *I.*
Inside starts with *I.*
Invisible and *invitation,*
They both start with *I.*

If You're Joyful

(sung to the tune of "If You're Happy and You Know It")

If you're joyful and you know it, [jump up high].
If you're joyful and you know it, [jump up high].
If you're joyful and you know it, then your actions surely show it.
If you're joyful and you know it, [jump up high].

Repeat the song, replacing the underlined phrase with dance a jig, *and* jog in place. *Then invite students to continue the song by creating other phrases featuring* J *words and actions.*

Judge Bear

Who knew there were so many *J*s to judge at the fair? Judge bear, of course!

Judge, judge,
Judge bear
Judged the contests
At the fair.

She judged the jams
And jellies too.
She sampled all;
There were quite a few.

She judged the riders
That jumped over things.
She judged the jeeps
That raced in a ring.

She judged the jitterbugs
That danced all day.
And she judged the jazz bands
That did swing and play.

She judged the jugglers
That juggled things high.
She judged the jets
That filled the sky.

Judge, judge,
Judge bear
Judged the contests
At the fair.

The Jet

Now boarding is this nonstop flight to *J* awareness! Before you sing with your youngsters, invite them to pretend their index fingers are jets and "fly" them each time they hear a *J* sound.

(sung to the tune of "My Bonnie Lies Over the Ocean")

The jet flew over the jungle.
The jet flew over the sea.
The jet flew over the mountain.
The jet flew over the tree.

Jet, jet, jet, jet
The jet flew over the sea-e-e.
Jet, jet, jet, jet
The jet just flew over me!

Jump for Jelly Beans

Sweeten *J* practice with this energetic letter-awareness song! Program a supply of large, colorful construction paper jelly beans with a variety of words that begin with *J* and some that begin with other letters. During a circle time, familiarize little ones with the song below, and then tell them that you want them to look for *J*. Sing the song together; then slowly cycle through the jelly bean words and have students jump for *J* words.

(sung to the tune of "Clementine")

Jump for jelly beans.
Jump for jelly beans.
Jump for jelly beans with *J.*
Just now jump for jelly beans.
Jump for jelly beans with *J.*

Jingle, Jingle

Invite a few children at a time to gently shake cluster bells or wrist bells as your whole class sings this song together. The perfect accompaniment to letter *J!*

(sung to the tune of "Are You Sleeping?")

Jingle, jingle. Jingle, jingle.
Jingle bells! Jingle bells!
I hear bells a-ringing,
Jing-a-ling-a-ling-ing.
Jingle bells! Jingle bells!

Jumping Jack

Encourage each youngster to pretend she is a jack-in-the-box while performing the words and movements in this fun action song.

(sung to the tune of "Are You Sleeping?")

Jumping Jack, Jumping Jack
Jumping up! Jumping back!
Hiding all the time
Until your box I wind.
Jumping Jack—out then back!

Jump from side to side with each beat.
Jump up high; then jump and crouch low.
Stay in a crouched position.
Pretend to wind an imaginary handle.
Jump up high; then jump and crouch low.

Let's Look for *K*s Today

(sung to the tune of "The Farmer in the Dell")

Let's look for *K*s today.
Let's look for *K*s today.
Heigh-ho, away we go.
Let's look for *K*s today.

Key starts with *K*.
Kitten starts with *K*.
Keyboard and *kindergarten*,
They all start with *K*.

K Sounds

This little ditty will engage your little ones while reinforcing the sound letter *K* makes.

(sung to the tune of "Jingle Bells")

K, K, K, K, K, K
Lots of *K*s around.
Everyone would like to know—
Just what is your sound?

/k/, /k/, /k/, /k/, /k/, /k/
/k/ is what we say.
Do you know any words
That start with letter *K*?

Children's chant:
Kite, kiss, and *kangaroo*
All start with *K;* yes, they do!

Repeat the song, substituting different K words in the chant.

34

Kick Your Feet

This active song is perfect to reinforce the /k/ sound while rousing your little sleepyheads after rest time. Be sure that each child has plenty of personal space and is lying on her back before beginning. Then invite children to gently kick their feet as described in the lyrics.

(sung to the tune of "Row, Row, Row Your Boat")

Kick, kick, kick your feet.
Kick your feet for *K*.
Kick them high.
Kick them low.
Kick them different ways.

Karate Bear

Karate, karate,
Karate bear
Has a blue belt
That he can wear.

He kicks for things
That start with *K*,
To protect *K* things
Day after day.

He kicks for kettles.
He kicks for keys.
He kicks for kites
Flying in the breeze.

He kicks for kitchens
And even kings.
He kicks for ketchup
Of all things.

Karate, karate,
Karate bear
Kicks for *K*s
To show he cares.

If You're Kind and You Know It

(sung to the tune of "If You're Happy and You Know It")

If you're kind and you know it, blow a kiss.
If you're kind and you know it, blow a kiss.
If you're kind and you know it, then your face will surely show it.
If you're kind and you know it, blow a kiss.

Continue with other verses that feature K such as "fly a kite" or "give a kick."

What Do You See?

The flowing rhythm of this poem will appeal to little ones as they focus on animals whose names begin with *K*.

Kangaroo, kangaroo under the tree,
Kindly tell us what you see.
I see a kookaburra in a tree.
I see a kookaburra up above me.

Kookaburra, kookaburra up in the tree,
Kindly tell us what you see.
I see a koala in a tree.
I see a koala next to me.

Koala, koala up in the tree,
Kindly tell us what you see.
I see a kangaroo under the tree.
I see a kangaroo under me.

"K-A-N-G-A!"

(sung to the tune of "Bingo")

This energetic little kangaroo will help raise *K* awareness while getting rid of the wiggles!

Verse: There is a kangaroo that [hops], and Kanga is her name-o.
Chorus: K-A-N-G-A, K-A-N-G-A, K-A-N-G-A, and Kanga is her name-o.

Repeat the song, substituting the underlined verb with knits, kicks, skips, *and so forth. Invite each child to perform the desired action as you sing the verse and chorus together.*

The Ls Are Leaping

Invite youngsters to perform some of the action words as they recite these lyrics, which accentuate *L* words!

(sung to the tune of "The Ants Go Marching")

Little [leaves] are leaping all around,
Some high, some low.
Large [leaves] are leaping all around,
Some high, some low.
Some go up, and some come down,
Spinning and swirling all over town.
Fluttering softly,
[Leaves] are leaping all around!

Repeat the song, replacing the underlined words with other L *words, such as* lizards, leprechauns, *and* lions.

I Love L!

(sung to the tune of "Three Blind Mice")

I love *L.*
I love *L.*
Yes, I do.
Yes, I do.

I love lions at the zoo.
I love lizards and llamas; do you?
I love licorice and lollipops too!
I love *L.*

Ladybug's Lunch

After your little ones have recited this poem, explain that ladybugs eat tiny bugs that live on leaves. Also have them listen for the /l/ sound at the beginning of *ladybug* and *leaf.* Give each child a leaf cutout and have her draw a few black dots for bugs, saying the /l/ sound as she draws each one. Finally, help each child glue a red pom-pom on her leaf for the ladybug. Munch, munch!

Once there was a ladybug,
Ladybug, ladybug.
Once there was a ladybug
Who landed on a leaf.

She stopped for a little lunch,
A little lunch, a little lunch.
She stopped for a little lunch.
Munch, munch, munch, munch, crunch!

Librarian Bear

Invite each youngster to make an L shape with his right hand, as shown, each time he hears a word that begins with the /l/ sound.

Librarian, librarian, librarian bear
Cares for books that she likes to share.

Books about lizards, lobsters, and bees.
Books about ladybugs landing on leaves.

Books about lazy lions and more.
Books about leopards and lambs galore!

Books about lemons, lettuce, and lunch.
Books about licorice and good things to munch.

Books about logs, lakes, and leaves.
Books about lands across the sea.

Librarian, librarian, librarian bear
Cares for books that she likes to share.

Lark's Song

Your little songbirds will enjoy performing the action described in the last line of each verse as you read this poem aloud. After reading the poem, ask each child to draw and color a picture of an animal whose name begins with the letter *L*. If desired, repeat the poem, replacing each animal and its action with youngsters' suggestions.

Larry the lizard
Listens to a lark.
Larry likes to hear its song
As he crawls in the dark.

Lucy the lion
Listens to a lark.
Lucy likes to hear its song
As she prowls in the dark.

Lenny the lobster
Listens to a lark.
Lenny likes to hear its song
As he swims in the dark.

Little Lizard

Your students will have lots of fun reciting this little rhyme and adding the fun actions. But don't limit your little ones! Ask them for more *L* word suggestions; then keep the verses coming!

Little lizard,
Little lizard,
What do you see?
I see a lobster
Looking at me.

Little lizard,
Little lizard,
What do you see?
I see a lion
Looking at me.

Little lizard,
Little lizard,
What do you see?
I see a ladybug
looking at me.

The Man in the Moon

After a few rousing rounds of this song to gain familiarity, separate students into two groups. Have the groups face each other, and then ask Group 1 to sing and act out the first verse, followed by Group 2 singing the second verse.

(sung to the tune of "The Muffin Man")

Have you seen the man in the moon,
The man in the moon, the man in the moon?
Have you seen the man in the moon?
He's watching over you.

Yes, I've seen the man in the moon,
The man in the moon, the man in the moon.
Yes, I've seen the man in the moon.
He can see you too!

The Mailman March

Invite your little tikes to march in place as you recite this song that celebrates the letter *M!*

(sung to the tune of "My Bonnie Lies Over the Ocean")

The mailman marched over a [marble].
The mailman marched over a [mop].
The mailman marched over the [marigolds],
To put my mail in the mailbox!

Mailman, mailman, delivering mail all day.
Mailman, mailman, lets nothing get in his way.

Repeat the song, replacing the underlined words with other M *words, such as* meadow, mountain, *or* moon.

The Moose Went Over the Molehill

Before reciting this fun song with youngsters, ask them to name *M* words. Record students' ideas on a chart to refer to later.

(sung to the tune of "The Bear Went Over the Mountain")

The moose went over the molehill.
The moose went over the molehill.
The moose went over the molehill.
What do you think she saw?

She saw a [mountain of money].
She saw a [mountain of money].
She saw a [mountain of money].
That is what she saw.

Repeat the song, replacing the underlined phrase with other M *phrases, such as* mound of mud, man in the moon, *or* messy mop.

Mama Mouse

As you read this poem to your little ones, ask them to show the sign language gesture for *M* each time they hear a word that begins with the letter *M*.

Mama mouse,
Mama mouse
Mixes mini muffins.

Mama mouse,
Mama mouse
makes milk shakes.

Mama mouse,
Mama mouse,
Where are the shakes and muffins?

Mama mouse,
Mama mouse—
She eats what she makes!

Motorcycle Bear

Your little cubs will memorize the /m/ sound after repeating this poem several times! After reading, ask each child to draw a picture of motorcycle bear doing an *M* activity. If desired, create a class book by stacking the pictures with a cover and stapling them together. It makes for mighty fine reading!

Motorcycle bear, motorcycle bear,
Motoring around without a care.

Motoring in the morning and midafternoon,
Making noise—vroom, vroom, vroom!

Motoring by [mountains], [meadows], and [moons].
Going and going, he really zooms!

Motorcycle bear, motorcycle bear,
Motoring around without a care.

Repeat the poem, replacing the underlined words with other M *words, such as* mailboxes, monkeys, *and* moose.

The *M* Café

After reading this poem, give each child a paper plate. Invite the child to draw her favorite food that begins with *M*. Then display the plates on an *M* display board covered in a plastic tablecloth.

Molly went to the *M* café,
And here's what the menu did say:

Muffins, marshmallows,
And macaroni too;
Milk shakes, melons,
And meatball stew.

Molly ordered a meal
Of meatball stew.
Then she munched some macaroni
And had a milk shake too!

Molly went to the *M* café.
I think she really enjoyed her stay.

Found a Necklace

After students become familiar with this song, invite them to take turns making up new verses with more *N* words.

(sung to the tune of "Clementine")

Found a new nest, found a new nest,
Found a new nest on the ground.
I put it back up in the tree,
Til the owner came around.

Found a necklace, found a necklace,
Found a necklace on the ground.
I gave it to a little girl
Who was looking all around.

Found a nut, found a nut,
Found a nut in a sack.
I gave it to a nutcracker
Who opened it with a crack!

Found a nose, found a nose,
Found a nose upside down.
I gave it to a silly man
Who was dressed up like a clown.

Nurse Bear

As you read this nurturing poem to youngsters, ask them to nod their heads each time they hear a word that begins with *N*.

Nurse, nurse,
Nurse bear,
Nursing others
With lots of care.

Changing nightgowns,
Putting on new sheets.
Wiping noses
And propping up feet.

Serving noodles,
Never making noise.
Reading nursery rhymes
To sleepy girls and boys.

Passing out nuts
For a nighttime treat.
Checking on little nappers
As they sleep.

Nurse, nurse,
Nurse bear,
Nursing others
With lots of care.

I Love N words

Before sharing this nifty song, ask students to name words that begin with *N*. Record youngsters' answers on a chart and then refer to the words as you repeat the song.

(sung to the tune of "Skip to My Lou")

I love *N* words; how about you?
I love *N* words; yes, I do.
I love *N* words. Here are a few:
Name, nine, and *neighbor* too!

Repeat the song, substituting other N *words, such as* note, nod, *and* nature.

name   nod
newt   note
noodle nine
number

I Looked in the Newspaper

After sharing the poem with your little detectives, give pairs of students a portion of a newspaper page (enlarge a copy if desired) and ask them to circle all the *N*s they spy.

I looked in the newspaper.
What did I spy?
Nine nifty *N* things
That I want to buy.

A nightgown, a nutcracker,
A necktie that's new.
A net and a nail
And a necklace for you.

A napkin, a nectarine,
A newt with spots!
Now it's off to the store,
To buy lots and lots!

Let's Look for *N*s Today

In advance, prepare several *N* picture cards for youngsters to hold up as the group recites the song.

(sung to the tune of "The Farmer in the Dell")

Let's look for *N*s today.
Let's look for *N*s today.
Heigh-ho, away we go.
Let's look for *N*s today.

Nest starts with *N*.
Neck starts with *N*.
Noodle, nose, and *number* too.
They all start with *N*.

O

I Like to Row for Short O

(sung to the tune of "My Bonnie Lies Over the Ocean")

I like to row in the river.
I like to climb up a tree.
I like to drive on the highway
To see short *O* things all around me.
O, O, O, O
I see short *O* things around me.
O, O, O, O
I see short *O* things around me.

I see otters in the water.
I see ostriches waving at me.
I see olives in the branches.
I see short *O*s all around me.
O, O, O, O
I see short *O* things around me.
O, O, O, O
I see short *O* things around me.

Repeat the song, substituting different short
O *words, such as* octopus *and* oxen.

O Sounds

Use all or part of this song to reinforce short *O* and long *O* sounds.

(sung to the tune of "Jingle Bells")

O, O, O, O, O, O
*O*s are all around.
We would all like to know—
What is *O*'s short sound?

/ŏ/, /ŏ/, /ŏ/, /ŏ/, /ŏ/, /ŏ/
/ŏ/ is what we say.
Do you know any words
That start the short *O* way?

Children chant:
Octopus, octagon, and *otter* too
Start with short *O;* yes, they do!

Repeat the song, substituting different short
O *words in the chant, or use the next verse to practice long* O.

O, O, O, O, O, O
*O*s are all around.
We would all like to know—
What is *O*'s long sound?

/ō/, /ō/, /ō/, /ō/, /ō/, /ō/
/ō/ is what we say.
Do you know any words
That start the long *O* way?

Children chant:
Open, over, and *oatmeal* too
Start with long *O,* yes they do!

Little Otter

This silly little nonsense poem will help your little ones focus on the short *O* sound. If desired, write the poem on a chart and have students circle or point to short *O* words.

I went walking down the street
When an otter I happened to meet.

He looked lost and all alone,
So I took that little otter home.

I gave him olives and an omelet too.
We watched a movie about an ostrich in a zoo.

I guess he'd had enough to eat
Because he ran right out on his little otter feet.

Then the little otter ran back to his home.
Now I'm the one feeling all alone!

Opposites All Around

Fit in this fun song during your short *O* study, and your youngsters will not only help you point out that *opposite* begins with short *O*, they'll also get a lesson in opposites!

(sung to the tune of "Twinkle, Twinkle, Little Star")

Opposites, opposites, all around.
When I have a smile, you have a frown.
When I go fast, you go slow.
When I say, "Stop," you say, "Go."
Opposites, opposites, all around.
When I stand up, you sit down.

O

I Love O words

(sung to the tune of "Skip to My Lou")

I love *O* words; how about you?
I love *O* words; yes, I do.
I love *O* words. Here are a few:
Ocean, open, and *overalls* too!

Repeat the song, substituting other long O *words, such as* Ohio, oar, *and* old.

Let's Look for O Today

(sung to the tune of "The Farmer in the Dell")

Let's look for *O* today.
Let's look for *O* today.
Heigh-ho, away we go.
Let's look for *O* today.

Oval starts with *O.*
Oatmeal starts with *O.*
Oak and *oat* and *overcoat—*
They all start with *O.*

If desired, change this song to feature short O *words. For added fun, bring in the* O *objects you plan to mention in the song, so students can point to each one when it's mentioned.*

Pound Play Dough

Sing this playful song with a small group of youngsters. Then invite them to act out each verse. Give each child a small ball of play dough and encourage her to perform the actions as you sing the song together. After you sing the song, help students recognize that each object they formed begins with the letter *P*. What other objects beginning with *P* can they make with play dough?

(sung to the tune of "Row, Row, Row Your Boat")

Pound, pound, pound your play dough.
Pound it as flat as can be.
Plop it on a plate. Oh!
A pancake now you see.

Roll, roll, roll your play dough.
Roll it like a snake.
Pinch a point into one end.
A pencil you did make!

Shape, shape, shape your play dough.
Shape it like a ball.
Add a stem; then look again—
A pumpkin for the fall!

Pancake Man

Your little bakers will eat up this silly pancake-making song! Sing the song with youngsters several times, each time substituting a different *P* ingredient for the underlined words. Then give each child a construction paper pancake and have her draw her favorite perfect pancake ingredient!

(sung to the tune of "The Muffin Man")

Oh, do you know the pancake man,
The pancake man, the pancake man?
Oh, do you know the pancake man
Who makes [pickle] pancakes?

Oh, yes, we know the pancake man,
The pancake man, the pancake man.
Oh, yes, we know the pancake man
He makes [pickle] pancakes!

Penny Purchase

In advance, have each child find and cut out a magazine picture that begins with the /p/ sound. Then ask your students to sit in a circle holding their pictures. Recite the poem several times; each time ask two volunteers to show and name their *P* pictures in place of the underlined words.

I have a penny. What can I buy?
A picture, a pickle, or a pizza pie.

I have a penny. What can I get?
Some popcorn, a pillow, or a new pink pet.

I have a penny. What will I do?
Purchase some [plums] and a [puzzle] for you.

Pilot Bear

What does pilot bear see from way up in the air? Little ones are glad to offer their suggestions, which will come in handy as you expand on this simple rhyme. In advance, copy the poem onto chart paper. Write students' suggestions of *P* words on individual sticky notes. As you reread the poem, place students' words over the underlined words in the poem.

Pilot bear, pilot bear
Flying high up in the air.

Flying over [parks] and [porches].
Flying all around.
Flying over [pools] and [pastures].
What else has he found?

Pretty Package

Everyone likes to get presents and packages—especially little ones! Before reading this poem, fill a box with one or more items that begin with *P*. Then wrap the box as if it arrived in the mail addressed to your class. To build excitement, bring out the package just before reading the poem. Then share the poem and have students guess the contents of the package before having them unwrap it and reveal the surprise.

A pretty package at my door.
A pretty package from a store.

Is it a present, just for me?
I think I'll peek, so I can see.

I tear off the paper and peek inside.
It's a pink piggy bank—what a surprise!

Let's Look for *P*s Today

(sung to the tune of "The Farmer in the Dell")

Here's a simple song that's perfect for building vocabulary! Ask youngsters to list words that begin with *P* and record their answers on a chart. Repeat the song, substituting students' words for the underlined words.

Let's look for *P*s today.
Let's look for *P*s today.
Heigh-ho, away we go.
Let's look for *P*s today.

Puppy starts with *P*.
Pig starts with *P*.
[Potato] and *[pumpkin]*,
They both start with *P*.

P

peas

popcorn

pizza

pig

potato

pear

I Like Q

(sung to the tune of "Three Blind Mice")

I like *Q*.
I like *Q*.
Yes, I do.
I like *Q*.

Q is for *quick* and *Q* is for *queen*.
Q is for *quilt* that is the color green.
Q is for *quarterback* on a team.
I like *Q*.
Yes, I do!

A queen!

Asking Questions

Little ones have all the answers when you assist them in reciting this chant! If desired, make a set of cards with the following pictures: a quarterback, a queen, a quail, and a duck quacking. After reciting each question, hold up the appropriate card and help students identify the picture. When children become proficient at this activity, invite a child to choose and hold the picture cards!

Question, question number one:
Who throws footballs in the sun?
A quarterback!

Question, question number two:
Who has a crown with jewels of blue?
A queen!

Question, question number three:
Whose nest is not in a tree?
A quail!

Question, question number four:
What does a duck say when it wants more?
"Quack!"

A Song About Q

Celebrate the letter *Q* with this catchy sing-along! Before introducing the song to your youngsters, explain that the word *recite* means to say something out loud.

(sung to the tune of "If You're Happy and You Know It")

Here's a little song about the letter *Q*.
There are words that start with *Q;* I'll list a few.
Quarter, quilt, quack, and *quite.*
There are more we could recite.
Here's a little song about the letter Q.

Queen Bear

The result of this royal poem and activity is a class full of smiling students! Write each line of the poem on a sentence strip, leaving a blank space each time the letter *Q* is used. Display the strips in order in a pocket chart. Then read the poem to your youngsters without the *Q*s. When the giggling subsides, explain to the students that the *Q*s are missing and need to be written in. Encourage children to observe closely as you write the missing letters. Finally, recite the corrected poem with your class!

Queen bear sits on her throne,
Counting her quarters all alone
Under a quilt made with golden thread,
With a queenly crown upon her head.

Four Quiet Queens

Spotlight the letter *Q* with this quirky chant about four quiet queens!

Four quiet queens sit all day,
Trying to think of something to say.
They quietly quilt till it's time to quit
Then they quickly eat a banana split!

Q and U

Use this poem to introduce youngsters to the partnership between the letters *Q* and *U*.

Q and *U* like each other a lot.
You'll find them together more often than not.
Quarter and *quiet, quilt* and *queen*
Are some of the words in which they're seen!

R

Red Robin

This rhyme is perfect for some springtime practice of the /r/ sound. Wrap up a reading of this rhyme with an outdoor walk to search for more *R* things.

Red robin, red robin
Up in the tree,
Name some *R* things
That you see.

I see rivers,
Rocks, and rainbows.
I see roosters
That like to crow.

I see raccoons,
Rabbits, and rats.
I see roses
And red rubber mats.

Red robin, red robin
Up in the tree,
Thank you for naming
Some *R* things for me.

Rancher Randy

Gather some bandanas or cowboy hats for your little ones when you introduce this song! Then send them galloping around the classroom on their pretend horses as they sing out a rousing round of this tune. Don't forget to rope in a beginning /r/ sound reminder as you introduce the song. Ride on!

(sung to the tune of "Yankee Doodle")

Rancher Randy came to town
For the rodeo.
He could ride, and he could rope.
He put on quite a show.

Round and round the ring he went.
Round and round he'd go.
He wore a hat and boots and chaps,
Dressed right from head to toe!

55

Noisy Robot

This little robot has quite a time staying upright when he bumps into many things, causing him to call out, "/r/!" Things aren't so good for the silly robot, but it is a great chance to remind your youngsters about the beginning sound /r/.

A rattling red robot
With round button eyes
Would often fall down
And then let out a cry!

Each time he bumped something,
He fell down.
"/r/," said the robot
As he landed on the ground!

"/r/," said the robot
as he bumped into a rock.
"/r/," said the robot
as he bumped into the clock.

"/r/," said the robot,
as he bumped into the rack.
"/r/" said the robot,
"Help! I landed on my back."

From Rubbish to Recycled

I looked through the rubbish,
And what can I say.
Lots of *R* things were thrown away.

Ribbons and ropes and radios,
Roller blades with crunched-up toes.
Raincoats, rattles, and rickrack galore.
Rakes and rowboats without oars.

It seems like a shame
To just toss them away.
Maybe we could recycle today!

Rainbow's Rows

Use the repetition of the word *rainbow* in this song to reinforce the beginning /r/ sound. While you're at it, there's plenty of practice with color words too.

(sung to the tune of "Row, Row, Row Your Boat")

Rainbow, rainbow,
Purple and blue.
Rainbow, rainbow,
Look, there's green too!

Rainbow, rainbow,
Yellow I see.
Rainbow, rainbow,
Orange and red—pretty!

Riddle Rhymes

Your students just might want to create *R* riddles of their own after solving this first round!

Here are some riddles that also rhyme.
Can you guess each answer in record time?

In case you have trouble, here's a hint:
The answers are *R* words; that should help a bit.

The first one you tie, or you coil it round.
It's helpful to keep a tent tied to the ground.   *(rope)*

The next is real fast as it soars through space.
Astronauts might be found in this place.   *(rocket)*

This last one is wet when it falls from the sky.
You'll need an umbrella to keep you dry.   *(rain)*

I'm a Little Sailboat

(sung to the tune of "I'm a Little Teapot")

I'm a little sailboat,
Short and stout.
I have a sail
That moves about.

When I go out sailing,
I soak in the sun,
Seeking the sea
And its salty fun!

Sing a Song of Six Seals

(sung to the tune of "Sing a Song of Sixpence")

Sing a song of six seals
Sitting on the sand.
Sixty-seven seagulls
Coming in to land.

When the seals look up
Into the sky,
The 67 seagulls
Just pass right by.

Sailor Bear

Ahoy there! Sailor bear is ready to sail into *S* practice!

Sailor, sailor, sailor bear,
Sailing his ship everywhere.

Sailing by seashells
On soft white sand.
Sailing by seagulls
And a lemonade stand.

Sailing by surfers
Out in the sun.
Sailing by seals
Having fun.

Sailing by sharks
And seaweed galore.
Sailing by sunbathers
Sitting on the shore.

Sailor, sailor, sailor bear
Sailing his ship everywhere.

Surfing

Surf's up! Encourage youngsters to pretend to paddle their surfboards out into the surf to catch a wave of *S* practice. Then invite children to sing together as they surf to shore. Hang ten!

(sung to the tune of "My Bonnie Lies Over the Ocean")

The surfer is out in the surf.
The surfer is out in the sea.
The surfer is out on his surfboard.
The surfer is little old me.
Surfing, surfing,
Surfing out on the sea, the sea.
Surfing, surfing,
The surfer is little old me!

S

A Sunflower Grows

Plant some *S* awareness when you recite this energetic poem with your little ones. Invite each child to perform the actions as you say the poem together. Then read the poem again with extra emphasis on the words that begin with *S*.

A sunflower starts with a tiny seed.
Soil, sun, and water
Are what it needs.
A sunflower sprouts
From something small
To something strong
And straight and tall.

Crouch down small like a seed.

Pretend to pat soil around feet.

Kneel with arms out.

Stand tall, arms out.

The Sandwich Song

Sing a silly sandwich song to reinforce *S* awareness whenever there's a spare second before snacktime! Sounds scrumptious!

(sung to the tune of "I'm a Little Teapot")

I'm a little sandwich on your plate.
I have something special, just you wait.
Is it [salami]? Is it ham?
Can you guess just what I am?

Repeat the song, substituting the underlined word with different S words—the sillier, the better!

Ten Little Toes

Program a sticky dot with the letter *T* for each child. Have each youngster remove her shoes and socks and then place a programmed sticky dot on her index finger. As the song is sung, have each child use her finger to point to and count her toes.

(sung to the tune of "Ten Little Indians")

One little, two little, three little toes,
Four little, five little, six little toes,
Seven little, eight little, nine little toes,
Ten toes on my feet.

Teddy Bear

Recite this rhyme once and your cubs will be ready to act it out the second time through!

Teddy, teddy, teddy bear,
He likes to exercise anywhere.

He likes to tap all of his toes.	*Tap toes.*
He likes to touch the tip of his nose.	*Touch nose.*
He likes to turn himself around.	*Turn around.*
He likes to tumble to the ground.	*Drop down to the floor.*
He likes to tiptoe way up high.	*Tiptoe.*
He like to toss things to the sky.	*Pretend to toss a ball in the air.*
He likes to tunnel under a chair.	*Pretend to crawl under a chair.*
He likes to exercise anywhere!	

She'll Be Towing with Her Tugboat

Grab your toy tugboats (or blocks for pretend tugboats) and have youngsters use them to practice forming the letter *T* on the floor after singing this little ditty!

(sung to the tune of "She'll Be Coming Round the Mountain")

She'll be [towing with her tugboat] when she comes.
She'll be [towing with her tugboat] when she comes.
She'll be [towing with her tugboat],
She'll be [towing with her tugboat],
She'll be [towing with her tugboat] when she comes.

Repeat the song, substituting turning in her taxi *in each line of the song.*

Tiger Song

Little ones will have a growlin' good time singing this tune! As you sing the song in the same manner as "Bingo," have children say the /t/ sound instead of clapping as a substitute for each of the letters.

(sung to the tune of "Bingo")

Deep in the jungle lives a cat,
And Tiger is his name-o.
T-I-G-E-R, T-I-G-E-R, T-I-G-E-R,
And Tiger is his name-o.

/t/, /t/, /t/

Ticktock

Get ready to hear the /t/ sound 60 times over! After singing this song, have each child watch the second hand on a large clock and say the /t/ sound with each tick of the hand.

(sung to the tune of "Are You Sleeping?")

"Tick, tick, tock,
Tick, tick, tock,"
Says the clock,
Says the clock.
/t/, /t/, /t/, /t/, /t/, /t/
/t/, /t/, /t/, /t/, /t/, /t/
Tick, tick, tock,
Tick, tick, tock.

Teacher Bear

There's a whole lot of teaching going on after reading this rhyme. Invite each youngster to "teach" the class how to write the letter *T,* describing the strokes as he writes.

Teacher, teacher,
Teacher bear,
Teaching students
About the sun, moon, and air.

Teaching about numbers
And our ABCs.
Teaching about fun stuff,
Like writing *T*s.

Teacher, teacher,
Teacher bear,
Teaching students
Everywhere!

U Sounds

These kid-pleasing lyrics will draw students' attention to both the long and short *U* sounds.

(sung to the tune of "Jingle Bells")

U, U, U, U, U, U
*U*s are all around.
We would all like to know—
What is *U*'s short sound?

/ŭ/, /ŭ/, /ŭ/, /ŭ/, /ŭ/, /ŭ/
/ŭ/ is what we say.
Do you know any words
That start the short *U* way?

Children's chant:
Under, up, and *uncle* too
Start with short *U*; yes, they do!

Repeat the song, substituting different short U *words in the chant, or use the next verse to practice long* U.

U, U, U, U, U, U
*U*s are all around.
We would all like to know—
What is *U*'s long sound?

/ū/, /ū/, /ū/, /ū/, /ū/, /ū/
/ū/ is what we say.
Do you know any words
That start the long *U* way?

Children's chant:
Use, unit, and *ukelele* too
Start with long *U*; yes, they do!

Umbrella Song

Sit under an open an umbrella while you share this cheery tune with youngsters. Then turn over the umbrella and pass around a bowl filled with a class supply of die-cut alphabet letters (be sure to include plenty of *U*s). Invite each child to take a letter and name it. If it's a *U,* encourage her to place it in the umbrella. If it's another letter, have her place it in her lap. Continue in this manner until each child has had a turn and the bowl is empty.

(sung to the tune of "I'm a Little Teapot")

Here's my new umbrella,
Wide and high.
It keeps me cozy, warm, and dry.
If the rain starts falling from the sky,
Just open it up, and you'll stay dry!

My Uncle

Short *U* is Uncle Upton's favorite sound! When students are familiar with this poem, invite them to make the sign for *U,* as shown, each time they hear the short *U* sound.

Uncle Upton walked under a bridge.
Uncle Upton sat under a tree.
Uncle Upton carried an umbrella
And kept all the rain off me!

The Unicorn

Share this poem with students; then invite each child to pretend she is a unicorn by putting her index finger on her head to resemble a horn. Then have her use her horn to point out examples of *U* in your classroom. How useful!

under

There once was a horse
Who was old and gray.
He wanted to look different
Somehow, someway.

He wished he were white
And knew how to fly.
He got his wish,
And he took to the sky.

His coat is now white.
On his head is a horn.
He has two wings.
He's a unicorn!

I Love *U* words

Introduce your students to words that begin with short *U* using this short, familiar tune.

(sung to the tune of "Skip to My Lou")

I love *U* words; how about you?
I love *U* words; yes, I do.
I love *U* words. Here are a few:
Up, umpire, and *umbrella* too!

*Repeat the song, substituting other short
U words.*

Let's Look for *U* Today

(sung to the tune of "The Farmer in the Dell")

Let's look for *U* today.
Let's look for *U* today.
Heigh-ho, away we go.
Let's look for *U* today.

Unload starts with *U.*
Upstairs starts with *U.*
Umbrella and *underwear,*
They both start with *U.*

My Valentine

As you sing this song to youngsters, ask them to give a thumbs-up each time they hear a *V* word.

(sung to the tune of "Three Blind Mice")

Valentine, valentine,
Please be mine; please be mine.
I'll play the violin for you.
I'll bring violets, oh so blue.
I'll wear a vest if you promise to
Be my valentine!

The Letter V

Encourage each child to write the letter *V* in the air with her index finger as you share this poem.

Can you make the letter *V?*
It's as easy as can be.
Slant line down,
Slant line up.
Very good *V!*

My Very *V* Vacation

Gather some *V* picture cards to incorporate with this song. Have youngsters sit in a circle and sing the song. Then show them two picture cards at a time to replace the underlined words as you repeat the song.

(sung to the tune of "My Bonnie Lies Over the Ocean")

Last summer we went on vacation.
My dad drove our van down the road.
We traveled down to a valley,
Then to a volcano we rode.
V, V, V, V
Vacationing is for me, for me.
V, V, V, V
There is so much to see.

The van drove past some villages.
We stopped at a very nice town.
I bought some [vases] and [violins],
And a violet velvet gown.
V, V, V, V
Vacationing is for me, for me.
V, V, V, V
There is so much to see.

ON VACATION

I Love V words

(sung to the tune of "Skip to My Lou")

I love *V* words; how about you?
I love *V* words; yes, I do.
I love *V* words. Here are a few:
Violin, video, and *vegetables* too!

Village Adventure

Capture students' attention with this very *V*-filled verse!

Once in a village, on a dark, dark night,
I spied a very funny sight:

A vampire with a violet bat,
A vulture and a velvet cat,

Some volleyballs on twisty vines,
And a van full of valentines.

In this place with its silly scene,
Would you believe it was Halloween?

wish and wink

Wishing and winking entice youngsters to stay on task as they learn the /w/ sound! Encourage students to wink each time they hear the /w/ sound as you sing the song. Then ask youngsters to list other *W* words and write them on a wish word wall. Repeat the song, replacing each underlined word with a word from the word wall.

*(sung to the tune of
"My Bonnie Lies Over the Ocean")*

I wish I had three wishes.
I know just what I would do.
If I had three wishes,
I'd wish for *W*s!

Wink, wink, wink, wink,
I'd wish for [watches], [wagons], and [worms].
Wink, wink, wink, wink,
They all begin with *W!*

walrus
watercolor
woodchuck
wave
weeds

window watch

Encourage youngsters to perform the action words as you recite this poem.

I washed the window and what did I see?
A wide-eyed walrus staring at me.

I watched him waddle and wiggle.
I watched him wash in the waves.
I watched him dive in the water,
And then I watched him wander away.

70

wave for the waiter

Your little waiters and waitresses will enjoy the wild *W* menu in this poem. In advance, create several word picture cards with *W* words such as *watermelon, weeds, worm, water, watch,* and *wagon.* Read the poem aloud to students. Then show them two picture cards and repeat the poem, replacing the underlined words each time. Just for fun, have two students at a time act out the poem.

I wave for the waiter.
I don't like to wait.
I am very, very hungry
And there's nothing on my plate.
"What do you wish?"
Asked the waiter at last.
"I'll have [waffles] with [walnuts],
And please make it fast!"

I'll Be Riding on a wave

Encourage youngsters to name *W* words to replace the underlined word, such as *windmill, walrus, washing machine,* and *wooden boat.*

(sung to the tune of "She'll Be Coming Round the Mountain")

I'll be riding on a [wave],
When I come.
I'll be riding on a [wave],
When I come.
I'll be riding on a [wave].
I'll be riding on a [wave].
I'll be riding on a [wave].
When I come.

wiggles

Get the wiggles out with this fun fingerplay. Encourage youngsters to move the corresponding body part(s) as they wiggle their way to quiet time.

I wiggle my fingers;
I wiggle my toes.
I wiggle my shoulders;
I wiggle my nose.
Now no more wiggles are left in me,
So I'm as still as I can be.

Little wiggle worm

Your little wiggle worms will be ready to learn after several renditions of this active poem.

(sung to the tune of "I'm a Little Teapot")

I'm a little wiggle worm;	*Wiggle body.*
Watch me go!	
I can wiggle fast	*Wiggle fast.*
Or very, very slow.	*Wiggle slow.*
I wiggle all around,	*Wiggle and turn around.*
Then back I go,	
Down to the ground	*Wiggle and bend down low.*
To the home I know.	

X-Ray Bear

Gather all your little doctors and show them a real X ray to introduce this extra special rhyme.

X-ray bear,
X-ray bear,
She looks at X rays
For breaks and tears.

She takes a picture
Of your body inside.
She takes a picture
Where nothing can hide.

She looks at your bones.
Does she see a break?
She knows from the X rays
What treatment to make.

Xs and Os

Chances are some of your youngsters already know about *X*s and *O*s, so let them reveal the special symbols of love to the class. As you recite the poem, ask a small group of students to use their bodies to form an X shape. Then give each child a sheet of construction paper to create a special XOXO card for a loved one.

A card came in the mail today.
It's filled with *X*s and *O*s.
I wish I knew just what they mean.
Does anybody know?

X means kisses.
O means hugs.
When you get them,
The card's filled with love.

X Marks the Spot

X marks the spot for exercise fun! In advance, make a class set of *X* puppets similar to the one shown. Then have each child use a puppet to gently tap the appropriate body part as you recite the poem.

X marks the spot,
Head, shoulder, toes.

X marks the spot,
Tummy, knee, nose.

X marks the spot,
Foot, heel, elbows.

X marks the spot—
Now everyone knows!

Ox with a Box

Introduce youngsters to words that *end* with *X* with this excellent poem! To prepare, write the poem on a chart. Read the poem as you point to each word. Then give a child a highlighter to mark each word that ends with *X.* Put the chart at a center for students to read and write the -*x* words.

This is the ox
Who has a box.
An ox with a box is he.
Inside the box he has a fox,
A fox for all to see!

yarn for Sale

Bring out some balls of yarn in a variety of colors to help this poem come to life. Use colored tape to mark a *Y* on each one. After students are familiar with the poem, encourage some volunteers to each hold a ball of yarn. Read the poem again. When a word is read that begins with *Y,* have them hold the balls of yarn high and then lower them again.

Yarn for sale, yarn for sale,
Yellow, red, green, and blue.
Yarn for sale, yarn for sale,
Some for me and some for you.

Enough to make a sweater
Or a scarf in blue and green.
Or maybe yellow slippers,
Nicest that I've ever seen.

yo-yo Bear

Give your students a demonstration of a yo-yo in action. Small as it is, it's difficult to keep it moving all the time. After an intentionally fumbled demonstration, read the poem aloud and then point out how talented yo-yo bear is to be able to yo-yo *anywhere.* Finally, mention how talented your students are at finding the /y/ sound in words they hear. Can they find some *Y*s in this poem? You bet!

Yo-yo bear, yo-yo bear,
He can yo-yo anywhere!
On a couch or on a chair,
Over here or over there!
Yo-yo bear, yo-yo bear,
He can yo-yo anywhere!

yawn!

Involve your students in singing this animated song and you know they'll pick up on the /y/ sounds as they yawn their way to the end of the tune.

(sung to the tune of "My Bonnie Lies Over the Ocean")

At night when it's dark and I'm sleepy,
When my bedtime story is read,
I yawn 'cause I'm feeling so tired,
Which means it's time to go to bed.
Yawn, yawn, it's time for me to go to bed, to bed!
Yawn, yawn, it's time for me to go to bed!

Raise arms as if yawning.
Raise arms as if yawning.

The Letter Y

(sung to the tune of "There's a Hole in the Bucket")

There's a letter named *Y*,
Named *Y*, named *Y*.
There's a letter named *Y*,
Oh, where is it found?

Well, it's found in *yard*.
And *yogurt* and *yawn*.
And it's found in *yellow*,
And /y/ is its sound!